# Minnesota

**BY JANE VERNON**

**CONTENT CONSULTANT**
Jacob Jurss, PhD
Professor of History
University of Saint Thomas

An Imprint of Abdo Publishing
abdobooks.com

abdobooks.com

Published by Abdo Publishing, a division of ABDO, PO Box 398166, Minneapolis, Minnesota 55439.

Core Library™ is a trademark and logo of Abdo Publishing.

Printed in the United States of America, North Mankato, Minnesota.
052022
092022

THIS BOOK CONTAINS RECYCLED MATERIALS

Cover Photo: Shutterstock Images, map and icons, Spoonbridge and Cherry; Michel Legault/ Shutterstock Images, loons
Interior Photos: Lasse Holst Hansen/Shutterstock Images, 4–5, 43; Red Line Editorial, 7 (Minnesota), 7 (USA); Newberry Library/Superstock/Alamy, 10–11; North Wind Picture Archives/AP Images, 13; Shutterstock Images, 15 (flag), 27, 41; Brian Lasenby/Shutterstock Images, 15 (bird); RLS Photo/ Shutterstock Images, 15 (fish); Edgar Lee Espe/Shutterstock Images, 15 (flower); Ted Kinsman/ Science Source, 15 (tree); Jacob Boomsma/Shutterstock Images, 19, 32, 45; David Brickner/ Shutterstock Images, 20–21; Karla Caspari/Shutterstock Images, 23; Danita Delimont/Shutterstock Images, 25; Jay Paull/Archive Photos/Getty Images, 28; Don Smetzer/Alamy, 28–29; Minnesota Historical Society/Corbis Historical/Getty Images, 34–35; Ross Marino/Icon and Image/Michael Ochs Archives/Getty Images, 37; Jerry Holt/Star Tribune/AP Images, 39

Editor: Angela Lim
Series Designer: Joshua Olson

**Library of Congress Control Number: 2021951404**

**Publisher's Cataloging-in-Publication Data**

Names: Vernon, Jane, author.
Title: Minnesota / by Jane Vernon
Description: Minneapolis, Minnesota : Abdo Publishing, 2023 | Series: Core library of US states | Includes online resources and index.
Identifiers: ISBN 9781532197642 (lib. bdg.) | ISBN 9781098270407 (ebook)
Subjects: LCSH: U.S. states--Juvenile literature. | Midwest States--Juvenile literature. | Minnesota--History--Juvenile literature. | Physical geography--United States--Juvenile literature.
Classification: DDC 977.6--dc23

Population demographics broken down by race and ethnicity come from the 2019 census estimate. Population totals come from the 2020 census.

# CONTENTS

CHAPTER ONE

# THE NORTH STAR STATE

Tourists stop along the North Shore Scenic Drive. The road starts in Duluth, Minnesota, and runs along the North Shore of Lake Superior. It eventually reaches Grand Portage, which is near the Canadian border.

Along Lake Superior, there are many scenic views of waterfalls and rocky cliffs. Each season brings new activities. People who take the drive during the fall see colorful autumn leaves along the Superior Hiking Trail. During the

Split Rock Lighthouse is one of many scenic destinations along Minnesota's North Shore.

## MINNESOTA'S MOTTO

**The French phrase *L'Étoile du Nord* means "Star of the North." It became the state motto in 1861. At that time Minnesota was the northernmost US state. The motto pays respect to Minnesota's early French Canadian settlers. Explorers used the North Star to navigate. Over time the motto came to symbolize that Minnesota is a leader for other states.**

winter, tourists can ski, snowshoe, and go ice fishing. Spring visitors enjoy wildflower blooms. They can boat and fish during the summer. Minnesota, the North Star State, offers much to see and do.

## ABOUT MINNESOTA

Minnesota is in the Midwest region of the United States. Canada borders it to the north. Lake Superior and Wisconsin lie to the east. Iowa forms the southern border. North and South Dakota are to the west. Saint Paul is the capital city. Minneapolis is directly west of the capital. It is the most populated city in the state. Saint Paul and Minneapolis are collectively called the Twin Cities. Duluth is another

# MAP OF MINNESOTA

Minnesota is famous for its lakes. How does this map help you understand Minnesota waterways? What else does the state have to offer?

major city. The Mayo Clinic in Rochester is one of the world's largest and most famous medical centers. The Mall of America in Bloomington is North America's largest shopping mall.

In addition to large cities, Minnesota is known for its natural landscapes. The state is sometimes called the Land of 10,000 Lakes. The state actually has more than 11,000 lakes. Minnesota's name comes from the Dakota word *Mnisota*, which means "the land where the waters reflect the sky." From nature to city life, there is something for everyone in Minnesota.

## PERSPECTIVES

### THE TWIN CITIES

**Many people love life in the Twin Cities. Travis Smith is a dean at the University of Minnesota in Minneapolis. He says, "It's certainly cold here during the winter months but it's not as bad as I expected it to be when I moved here from Chicago. People in the Twin Cities don't let the weather dictate their lives. They get out and enjoy all the outdoor activities the cities have to offer year-round."**

# STRAIGHT TO THE SOURCE

**Minnesota lakes attract fishers hoping to haul in a big catch. In a Minnesota travel guide, Jess Myers reflected on the Lake of the Woods near his hometown of Warroad. He wrote:**

> *As a small-town Warroad kid who loved fishing, the shore of Lake of the Woods felt like the bustling center of the universe on a sunny June day. . . . Nicknamed the "Walleye Capital of the World," this massive body of water is one of the best fishing destinations, luring [fishers] from around the globe to seek out its legendary walleye. . . . On any given spring, summer, or fall day, boats by the hundreds . . . can be seen across the Big Traverse and around the islands of the Northwest Angle as their occupants scramble to grab the landing net and haul in a trophy.*

Source: Jess Myers. "Lake of the Woods: Walleye Capital of the World." *Explore Minnesota*, 2021, exploreminnesota.org. Accessed 27 July 2021.

## WHAT'S THE BIG IDEA?

**Take a close look at this passage. What is the main connection being made between the Lake of the Woods and fishing? How does the passage help you understand how important fishing is in the region?**

CHAPTER TWO

# HISTORY OF MINNESOTA

People have lived in the Minnesota region for more than 12,000 years. Two American Indian nations made up the largest populations. The Dakota lived in villages throughout the state. The Ojibwe began to move to Minnesota from eastern North America about 1,500 years ago. They lived along the shores of Lake Superior. The Dakota and the Ojibwe sometimes fought and sometimes were allies. Both peoples grew and harvested wild rice. They also made maple

This image shows American Indians canoeing on Lake Itasca.

syrup from the sugar maples in the area. People of these nations still live in the state today.

## EUROPEAN EXPLORATION

In 1660 French explorers became the first Europeans in the Minnesota region. In 1682 René-Robert Cavelier, Sieur de La Salle claimed the Mississippi River system and the surrounding land for France. The land was called the Louisiana Territory. It included present-day Minnesota.

The French claimed the entire Minnesota region until the French and Indian War (1754–1763). American Indians fought on both sides as the French clashed with the British over land ownership. The British defeated the French. Land east of the Mississippi River, including eastern Minnesota, fell under British control.

Their control was short-lived. The United States won independence from Great Britain in the Revolutionary War (1775–1783). The land east of the Mississippi River was transferred to the new nation.

French missionaries arrived in the Minnesota region to spread Christianity to American Indians.

In 1787 the US government created the Northwest Territory, which included part of present-day Minnesota and five other states. The US government purchased the Louisiana Territory from France in 1803. Western Minnesota became part of the United States at that time.

## WARS AND CONFLICTS

Zebulon Pike led the first US expedition into the Minnesota region in 1805. Pike made a treaty with the Dakota to get approximately 100,000 acres (40,500 ha) of land. Pike wanted the land for military forts. The Dakota leaders present did not speak English. Interpreters may not have been clear about the treaty terms. Pike valued the land at $200,000, but the US government paid only $2,000 to the Dakota for their land.

By 1812 Great Britain was at war again with the United States. During the War of 1812 (1812–1814), American Indian nations such as the Dakota, the Ojibwe, and the Ho-Chunk sided with the British. Many American Indians were unhappy with the US settlers who had forced them from their lands. The war ended with the Treaty of Ghent, which established Minnesota's northern boundary.

Minnesota's population grew rapidly after the war. By 1858 more than 150,000 people lived in the region. Minnesota became the thirty-second US state on May 11, 1858.

Only a small area of land in Minnesota still belonged to the Dakota by 1862. Due to actions of the US government, the nation did not have the resources to survive. The Dakota launched attacks against

## MINNESOTA

# QUICK FACTS

Take a look at Minnesota's state symbols. How do they help you understand the state's geography? Are any of the symbols surprising?

**Abbreviation:** MN
**Nickname:** The North Star State
**Motto:** *L'Étoile du Nord* (The Star of the North)
**Date of statehood:** May 11, 1858
**Capital:** Saint Paul
**Population:** 5,706,494
**Area:** 86,936 square miles (225,163 sq km)

## STATE SYMBOLS

**State bird**
Common loon

**State flower**
Showy lady's slipper

**State fish**
Walleye

**State tree**
Norway pine

US settlers to defend their land. The Dakota and the US Army fought in the US–Dakota War of 1862. The Dakota fighters surrendered after six weeks. After the war, the US military sentenced more than 300 Dakota fighters to death. President Abraham Lincoln dismissed some of the sentences. But the US government killed 38 Dakota men for their involvement in the war. This was the largest mass execution in US history.

The US government removed the Dakota from their land and forced the people to live in a concentration camp at Fort Snelling. Hundreds died due to the harsh conditions. The US government later sent the Dakota to live on the Crow Creek Reservation in present-day South Dakota.

## THE 1900s AND BEYOND

Minnesota's population continued to grow. In the early 1900s, immigrants settled in the Saint Paul neighborhood of Rondo. By 1950 Rondo was home to approximately 85 percent of Saint Paul's

Black population. Other people in the Twin Cities wanted a highway to connect the two cities. This would cut Rondo in two. Rondo residents protested, but construction on the highway began in 1956. Today Black Minnesotans celebrate their culture in an annual festival called Rondo Days.

The Saint Lawrence Seaway opened in 1959. It connected the Great Lakes to the Atlantic Ocean.

## PERSPECTIVES

### THE JOURNEY TO FORT SNELLING

**The US Army forced 1,658 Dakota people to move to Fort Snelling. These people had not taken part in the US–Dakota War of 1862. But the Dakota faced violence from white settlers along the 150-mile (241-km) journey. American settlers threw rocks and boiling water at the Dakota. Fifty-seven Dakota people died along the journey. Ramona Kitto Stately's great-great-grandmother was one of the Dakota people who was forced into Fort Snelling. Staley reflected, "For the Dakota, this is not something that happened a long time ago. The wounds are very fresh."**

## MINNESOTANS IN OFFICE

**Many Minnesotans have held positions in the federal government. Pierce Butler became the first Minnesotan to serve on the US Supreme Court in 1923. Hubert Humphrey took office as vice president under Lyndon Johnson in 1965. Walter Mondale was vice president to Jimmy Carter from 1977 to 1981. In 2018 Ilhan Omar was elected to the US House of Representatives along with Rashida Tlaib from Michigan. They became the first two Muslim women in the US Congress. In the state government, Peggy Flanagan became the lieutenant governor in 2018. A White Earth Ojibwe, she became the nation's first American Indian woman to serve in that position.**

Minnesota industries grew as materials could be transported around the world from Duluth.

## GOVERNMENT

Minnesota's government has three branches. The legislative branch votes on new laws. The executive branch includes the governor, who signs or vetoes bills. The third branch is the judicial branch, which includes several court systems.

Minnesota also has 11 federally recognized

Approximately 35 million tons (32 million metric tons) of cargo pass through the Port of Duluth-Superior each year.

tribes, including seven Ojibwe bands and four Dakota communities. These nations each have their own governments and laws. Their government systems are separate from the state government.

## EXPLORE ONLINE

Chapter Two touches on the US–Dakota War of 1862. The article at the website below goes into more depth on the conflict. What information from the article backs up what you read in Chapter Two? What additional information did you learn about the US–Dakota War of 1862 from the article?

### THE US–DAKOTA WAR OF 1862: CAUSES OF THE WAR

abdocorelibrary.com/minnesota

CHAPTER THREE

# GEOGRAPHY AND CLIMATE

Rolling plains cover much of Minnesota. Glaciers created this landscape millions of years ago. Glaciers also helped form Minnesota lakes. They filled lowlands with water as they melted. Red Lake is a glacial lake. It is also the largest lake contained within the state.

In addition to its many lakes, Minnesota is home to the headwaters of the Mississippi River. The river begins in northern Minnesota.

Superior National Forest covers more than 3 million acres (1 million ha) in northern Minnesota.

From there it flows southward, eventually reaching the Gulf of Mexico.

The Sawtooth Mountains run along part of the North Shore. Eagle Mountain lies in this range. It stands at 2,301 feet (701 m) above sea level, the highest point in Minnesota. Superior National Forest also stretches across the north. The forest includes the Boundary Waters, a collection of lakes and other waterways that lie between Minnesota and Canada. Angle Inlet lies across these waters. This Minnesota town is the northernmost point in the United States outside of Alaska. Visitors must drive through Canada or sail across the Lake of the Woods to reach the inlet.

## CLIMATE

Minnesota is famous for its cold, snowy winters. Temperatures can fall to −30 degrees Fahrenheit (−34°C) in northern Minnesota. This region receives more than 70 inches (178 cm) of snow each year.

Waterfalls such as Minnehaha Falls can freeze during the winter.

Southwestern Minnesota receives an average annual snowfall of 35 inches (90 cm).

But Minnesota is not always cold. Summer temperatures can rise above 100 degrees Fahrenheit (38°C). The state also receives plenty of rainfall. Much of the rain falls during the growing season, which lasts from May to September.

## MINNESOTA WILDLIFE

Minnesota's weather and geography create habitats for many types of plants and animals. Minnesota lakes are home to fish such as walleyes, trout, and bass. Minnesota's state bird, the common loon, is also found in and near lakes. This aquatic bird dives underwater to hunt fish.

Norway pines often grow near lakeshores. These trees are good sources of lumber. Wildflowers such as the showy lady's slipper bloom in swamps and bogs. The lady's slipper is

### EMERALD ASH BORER

Invasive species are animals and plants that are introduced to an area where they do not naturally occur. They can have a huge impact on native wildlife. The emerald ash borer is an invasive beetle in Minnesota. Originally from Asia, the beetles were discovered in Saint Paul in 2009. The beetles feed on ash trees, which weakens and kills the trees. There are nearly 1 billion ash trees in Minnesota. Scientists are working to control the emerald ash borer population to protect these trees.

Timber wolves vary in color. They are often gray but can also be black or white.

Minnesota's state flower. The plant is slow-growing and can take 16 years to bloom for the first time.

Other animals and plants live in the state's forests. Animals such as white-tailed deer, moose, and black bears roam. Minnesota has the largest wolf population of any US state outside of Alaska. But there are fewer wolves in Minnesota today than there were in the past.

## PERSPECTIVES

### WOLVES IN MINNESOTA

**Gray wolves once roamed throughout the state. But European settlers killed wolves to protect their livestock. Wolf populations dwindled. People worked to make sure wolves did not go extinct. The wolf population has more than doubled since the 1970s, with approximately 2,600 wolves in 2020. The International Wolf Center reported, "Minnesotans clearly value wolves, viewing the animal as ecologically important, scientifically fascinating, [attractive], recreationally appealing, and significant for future generations."**

Superior National Forest is home to pine, fir, and spruce trees. Wildflowers such as aster and goldenrod grow throughout the forest. Chippewa National Forest is another major forest in Minnesota. Pine, birch, and maple trees are common in this forest. Native grasses such as big bluestem and prairie June grass cover the prairie regions of Minnesota.

Minnesota wildflowers attract many types of butterflies, including the monarch butterfly.

From April to October, a variety of colorful wildflowers are in bloom.

## FURTHER EVIDENCE

Chapter Three introduces some of the wildlife found in Minnesota. The article at the website below also describes the state's wildlife. Which plants and animals mentioned in Chapter Three are also mentioned in the article? What new information does the article give?

### A FIELD GUIDE TO MINNESOTA'S ICONIC ANIMALS

abdocorelibrary.com/minnesota

PILLSBURY
A
PILLSBURY
A

CHAPTER FOUR

# RESOURCES AND ECONOMY

Minnesota is one of the top-producing agricultural states in the nation. Sugar beets, corn, and kidney beans are some of Minnesota's top crops. Turkeys and hogs are important livestock.

Minnesota is also home to many food-related industries. In 1866 the first modern flour mill in the state opened at Saint Anthony Falls in Minneapolis. The food manufacturing companies General Mills and

The first Pillsbury flour mills opened in Minnesota in 1869. The company now produces baked goods including biscuits and cinnamon rolls.

## TOP TURKEY STATE

Minnesota has been the leading producer of turkeys in the United States since 1939. Minnesota turkey farmers raise more than 42 million turkeys each year. The turkey industry brings in $1 billion to the state and provides 26,000 jobs.

Jennie-O Turkey Store is headquartered in Willmar, Minnesota. In addition to whole turkeys, Jennie-O also produces turkey sausages and lunch meats. These foods are shipped worldwide.

Pillsbury can trace their origins to the Saint Anthony Falls flour mill. Today General Mills owns Pillsbury and is headquartered near Minneapolis. Hormel, Land O'Lakes, and Jennie-O are other food manufacturing companies in Minnesota.

Agricultural products can be used for fuel. Ethanol is a fuel made from corn. It produces less emissions than gasoline and is better for the environment. Gasoline can be blended with ethanol to make it less harmful.

Natural resources have long played an important role in the state. Minnesota produces more iron ore and taconite than any other US state. The Mesabi Iron Range in northern Minnesota has a mining history of more than 125 years. In 1951 Minnesota produced 82 percent of the US iron ore supply. Today workers mine a lower-quality iron ore called taconite. This material is used to make steel.

## PERSPECTIVES

### ELECTRIC VEHICLES

**Electric vehicles (EVs) do not create as much pollution as gas-powered vehicles. Experts predict that EV use will rise in the future. In 2021 Minnesota lawmakers passed the Clean Cars rule, which will make EVs more readily available. It also requires that new gas-powered vehicles run more efficiently. State senator Dave Senjem said of EVs, "I think we all understand that EV transportation is on its way. . . . It's the new way, and it will be with us sooner than we think."**

## OTHER INDUSTRIES

Over time Minnesota has developed a diverse economy. The headquarters for the manufacturing

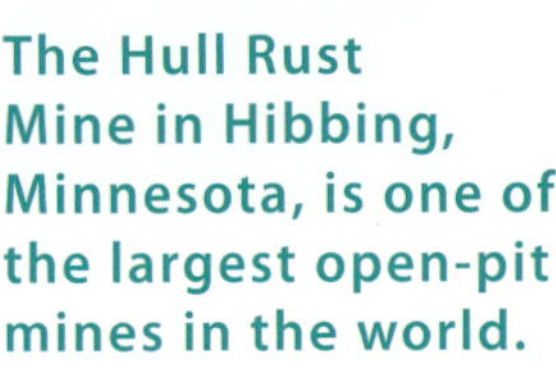

**The Hull Rust Mine in Hibbing, Minnesota, is one of the largest open-pit mines in the world.**

company 3M is near Saint Paul. It makes tape, Post-it notes, bandages, and many other products. Target was founded in Minnesota. Best Buy is headquartered in Richfield. The Mayo Clinic is in Rochester.

Approximately 11 percent of Minnesotans work in the tourism industry. Minnesota cities are popular tourist destinations. Outdoor adventures also attract visitors. The National Park Service recognizes six sites in Minnesota, including Voyageurs National Park. The park is near the Canadian border and includes scenic forests and lakes.

# STRAIGHT TO THE SOURCE

**Dr. William Mayo and his sons founded the Mayo Clinic in Rochester in 1914. His goal was to create a team of medical experts. He said:**

> ***The sum-total of medical knowledge is now so great and wide-spreading that it would be futile for one man to attempt to acquire, or for any one man to assume that he has, even a good working knowledge of any large part of the whole. . . . The best interest of the patient is the only interest to be considered, and in order that the sick may have the benefit of advancing knowledge, union of forces is necessary.***

**Source: Kate Roberts. "Mayo Clinic."** ***Minnesota Historical Society*****, 18 Mar. 2020, mnopedia.org. Accessed 28 July 2021.**

## CONSIDER YOUR AUDIENCE

**Adapt this quote for a different audience, such as younger friends or siblings. Rewrite the passage to convey the same information in language that they will more easily understand. How does your passage differ from the original text and why?**

CHAPTER FIVE

# PEOPLE AND PLACES

Many of Minnesota's earliest settlers were from Northern Europe. As a result, most of Minnesota's population is white. Approximately 79 percent of the population is non-Hispanic white. Black people make up 7 percent of the population. More than 5 percent of the population is Hispanic or Latino, and another 5 percent is Asian. More than 1 percent of the population is American Indian.

Writer F. Scott Fitzgerald, who was born in Saint Paul, and his wife, Zelda, pose near their home in Dellwood, Minnesota, in 1921.

Minnesota also has a high percentage of refugees. This includes many Somali and Hmong people. The state has the largest Somali population outside of Somalia. The Hmong have roots in ancient China. They began coming to Minnesota in 1975 to escape wars in Laos. Today the Twin Cities are home to many Hmong people.

## FAMOUS PEOPLE

The late musician Prince was one of Minnesota's famous residents. He was born in Minneapolis. Prince could play many different instruments. He wrote, recorded, and produced several albums. Today Prince's home, Paisley Park, in Chanhassen, is open to visitors.

Other famous Minnesotans include F. Scott Fitzgerald and Charles Schulz. Fitzgerald is best known for his novel *The Great Gatsby*. His home in Saint Paul is a national historic landmark. Schulz was born in Minneapolis and grew up in the Twin Cities. His iconic *Peanuts* cartoons ran for almost 50 years.

Prince performed onstage during his 1984 Purple Rain tour.

Gymnast Suni Lee is from Saint Paul. She competed in the Tokyo Olympics in 2021. Lee became the first Hmong American to win a gold medal in Olympic history.

## IMPORTANT PLACES

Minnesotans take advantage of the outdoors. There are miles of hiking trails throughout the state. Gooseberry Falls State Park is one of the most visited parks in Minnesota. It is located along the North Shore. People can stay active in the winter by snowmobiling

## PERSPECTIVES

### NORTHERN LIGHTS

**The northern lights, or aurora borealis, are natural events in which curtains of brightly colored light can be seen in the night sky. Particles from the sun react with Earth's atmosphere, causing the colors to appear. Minnesota's northern location makes it a good destination to see the lights. Photographer Travis Novitsky explains that Minnesota lakes add to the beauty. He says, "My favorite spot is on the south shore of any inland lake in northeast Minnesota. Being on the south shore means you get a great view of the lights looking north over the lake."**

and cross-country skiing. Visitors to Voyageurs National Park can camp, canoe or kayak, and stargaze.

Minnesota cities also offer many opportunities to explore the outdoors. Fort Snelling State Park is located in Saint Paul. The park has hiking and biking trails. Additionally many cities have lanes that allow bikers to travel safely alongside cars.

Minnesota also values the arts. The Children's Theatre Company (CTC) in Minneapolis is the country's

Hmong residents cheered for Suni Lee at a 2021 parade welcoming the Olympic champion. Some wore traditional clothing to celebrate.

largest theater for young people. It produces shows for young audiences. But people of all ages are welcome to watch performances at the CTC. Minneapolis is the site of the Walker Art Center, a modern art museum. It has a famous sculpture garden that showcases the *Spoonbridge and Cherry* fountain. The Guthrie Theater, founded in 1963 by English theatrical director Sir William Tyrone Guthrie, in Minneapolis is one of the first major resident theaters in the United States. Duluth is the birthplace of the famous musician Bob Dylan. Tourists flock to take pictures in front of Dylan's childhood home. The city hosts the Duluth Dylan Fest each year to celebrate him.

The Twin Cities host many major professional sports teams. Minnesota's major basketball, football, and baseball teams all play their games in downtown Minneapolis. The Minnesota Lynx have won four championships as of 2021.

In Saint Paul, fans can cheer for the Minnesota United soccer team and the Minnesota Wild hockey team. Many Minnesotans are passionate about hockey. Since joining the National Hockey League in 2000, the Wild have attracted some of the highest rates of attendance in the league.

## THE MINNESOTA STATE FAIR

**More than 2 million people attend the Minnesota State Fair each year. It has been a Minnesota tradition since before Minnesota became a state. First hosted in 1855, the fair educates guests in the best of Minnesota agriculture, art, and industry. The 12-day fair boasts nearly 500 types of food and more than 900 live shows. It is also called the Great Minnesota Get-Together.**

The *Spoonbridge and Cherry* fountain is an iconic sculpture in Minneapolis.

Hockey lovers travel to Eveleth, Minnesota, to visit the US Hockey Hall of Fame.

Minnesota is a beautiful state filled with outdoor adventures. The state boasts a large farming industry and important natural resources. Major cities have art museums, sporting events, and shopping malls. The North Star State is a leader in many ways.

# IMPORTANT DATES

**12,000 years ago**

The first people live in the Minnesota region.

**1787**

The US government creates the Northwest Territory, which includes part of present-day Minnesota.

**1805**

US explorer Zebulon Pike explores the Minnesota region. He signs a treaty with the Dakota.

**1858**

Minnesota becomes the thirty-second US state on May 11.

**1862**

The US–Dakota War of 1862 lasts for six weeks. Thirty-eight Dakota men are sentenced to death. The US Army forces the Dakota to live in a concentration camp at Fort Snelling before removing them from the state.

**1866**
The first modern flour mill in the state opens in Minneapolis.

**1914**
Dr. William Mayo and his sons found the Mayo Clinic in Rochester.

**1959**
The Saint Lawrence Seaway opens, connecting the Great Lakes to the Atlantic Ocean.

# STOP AND THINK

## Tell the Tale

Chapter One of this book describes many things to see and do along the North Shore Scenic Drive. Imagine you and your family are making the drive from Duluth to Grand Portage. Write a journal entry about your trip. What activities do you choose along the way? What sights do you see? Give plenty of details.

## You Are There

This book describes some of the popular tourist destinations in Minnesota. Imagine you are traveling through the state. Write a letter home telling your friends what you see and do. What places do you visit in the cities? What parks do you explore? Be sure to add plenty of detail to your notes.

## Surprise Me

Chapter Three discusses Minnesota wildlife. After reading this book, what two or three facts about plants and animals in Minnesota did you find most surprising? Write a few sentences about each fact. Why did you find each fact surprising?

## Another View

Chapter Two talks about the relationship between the Dakota and the US government in the early 1800s. As you know, every source is different. Ask a librarian or another adult to help you find another source about the 1805 Dakota Treaty. Write a short essay comparing and contrasting the new source's point of view with that of this book's author. What is the point of view of each author? How are they similar and why? How are they different and why?

# GLOSSARY

**concentration camp**
a place where an army or military holds a large number of people, especially those of a specific culture or religion

**emission**
a substance put forth into the air, such as smoke or a polluting gas

**execution**
the act of putting someone to death

**extinct**
no longer existing

**glacier**
a large body of ice that moves across land

**headquarters**
the business center of a company

**headwaters**
the source of a stream or river

**immigrant**
a person who moves to and lives in a new country

**resident theater**
a professional theater that puts on its own shows

**treaty**
an official agreement between governments

**veto**
to stop a bill from becoming a law

# ONLINE RESOURCES

To learn more about Minnesota, visit our free resource websites below.

Visit **abdocorelibrary.com** or scan this QR code for free Common Core resources for teachers and students, including vetted activities, multimedia, and booklinks, for deeper subject comprehension.

Visit **abdobooklinks.com** or scan this QR code for free additional online weblinks for further learning. These links are routinely monitored and updated to provide the most current information available.

# LEARN MORE

Ryan, Todd. *Minnesota Vikings*. Abdo, 2020.

Tekiela, Stan. *The Kids' Guide to Birds of Minnesota*. Adventure, 2018.

# INDEX



## About the Author

Jane Vernon is the author of more than 100 books for children, both nonfiction and fiction. Her favorite topics are nature; arts and crafts; food and cooking; biographies; health; survival; and science, technology, engineering, and math (STEM).